THOUGHT LEADERSHIP

THOUGHT LEADERSHIP

MERYDITH WILLOUGHBY

Copyright © 2020 by Merydith Willoughby

All rights reserved. No part of this publication may be reproduced, distributed, or transmitted in any form or by any means, including photocopying, recording, or other electronic or mechanical methods, without the prior written permission of the publisher, except in the case of brief quotations embodied in critical reviews and certain other noncommercial uses permitted by copyright law.

A catalogue record for this book is available from the National Library of Australia

www.linkedin.com/in/merydithwilloughby

Willoughby, Merydith (author)
Thought Leadership
ISBN 978-1-922452-61-0
Leadership / Thought Leader
Leadership / Inner Leader

Typeset Whitman 11/17

Edited by Green Hill Publishing
Cover image by Lightspring via Shutterstock
Cover and book design by Green Hill Publishing

For information on services and books contact:
Merydith Willoughby
Executive advisor
info@merydithwilloughby.com
New York City 718 790 9729
Australia 61 435086641

While the author has used her best efforts in preparing this book, she does not make any representation, whether implied or otherwise about the accuracy or completeness of the contents of this book or the application of the book's contents to the reader's personal situation. The information and strategies contained in this book may not be suitable for your situation and the author gives no advice as to what you should or should not do in relation to what is written in this book whatsoever. Any resemblance to actual persons or events is coincidental.

Contents

Thought Leadership … vii
Merydith Willoughby … ix
Books by the same author … xi

1 Nuts and bolts … 1
2 Upside down thinking … 15
3 Infrastructure … 29
4 New York City brain … 45
5 Incredible human machine … 59
6 Creative process … 73
7 John Lennons of the world … 91
8 Introspection … 109

Thought Leadership

As I traipse back through the centuries of information available outlining how humans have lived, been managed and controlled, I note with disappointment that while much positive change has occurred, much remains the same. This has become increasingly evident with the way human beings are manipulated into behaving in ways that suit institutions and other people's purposes. It remains a difficult - near impossible - task to unravel who you really are when there are generational systems in place, firmly embedded to keep you where you belong. These dominating forces - which are woven into the structure of every society, family, culture and generation, can see those of us who want to make change and understand who we are as a human being in the bigger picture, trip up at every intersection. The impact of this on humanity is behemothic. It can keep us locked into behaving like scared, small, dominated children throughout our whole life. When you think about the ramifications of this, you realise just how important it is for individuals to learn how to develop their inner leader and to think and behave like a thought leader. *Thought Leadership* proposes how this can be achieved; where we break down the layers of dominance and become aware of the invisible net that surrounds and controls us throughout every moment of our life. When we do this, we have the best chance of creating a more equitable society, community, family, generation, and individual life. We can then investigate who we really are and allow our true self to evolve. The impact on humankind with this approach to living would be phenomenal.

Merydith Willoughby

Travelling the world and talking to thousands of people over the years, I have learned much. It has become clear to me that most people think leadership is for the chosen few. Thinking and behaving like this alienates society and keeps citizens and humanity segregated and incarcerated. Every single person has an inner leader. Every single person can be taught how to think like a thought leader. The sooner we assist people to think and behave this way, the better. Better for them, better for their family and better for the global community. Having worked at all levels of society and having been an observer of the incredible human machine I have seen what is possible when people at all levels of ability are provided with nourishment and support. After all, it's just changing the cogs in our mind and challenging our social conditioning and giving our evolution a bit of a kick start, seeing it from a different viewpoint and then practising until we have embedded new ways of thinking and behaving. When the conversation deepens with these enlightening, interesting conversations and an inquiry is made as to what I do in my professional life, it is an opportunity to discuss leadership more deeply and given this is close to my heart, it can be a wide, interesting, fulfilling conversation. The response from an intergenerational mix is of interest and enthusiasm and support for these ideas but they haven't heard them spoken about this way. Their response is music to my ears. It inspires me. It gives me the enthusiasm and passion and energy to continue to unravel the incredible human machine and to continue talking about it globally, writing about it and speaking on the radio. It is a beautiful thing to see a light bulb go off in their mind and I often wonder what they take away from the conversation and how it impacts their life.

Books by the same author:
If it's to be: It's up to me
Back from Hell
Sex in the Boardroom
Thought Leadership

NUTS AND BOLTS

Thought Leadership is not about me. It is about you. It has been written for the specific purpose of sharing the knowledge I have acquired over many years. It has been designed to assist you to unpack who you are, to understand that the terms: inner leader and thought leader, are as relevant for you as they are for senior executives, presidents, governors, waged, non-waged, and people at any ability level.

I want you to know and learn how to step into your power and never, ever allow anyone or anything to take it away. To know that your past experience does not determine your future. To know that you determine your future every second of the day, every day of the year, every year of your life. When you falter - as we all do - you can pick yourself up, dust yourself off and get on with it, having learned from that experience.

I want you to know how important it is to stop, think about and reflect daily, weekly, monthly, yearly, as to how and where you are really going in your life. And to ask: does this reflect what you really want to do with your life, or are you just filling in time and doing what other people want you to do or what you think society expects and demands of you?

I want you to know how important it is to mentor yourself daily, weekly, monthly, yearly and to talk to yourself and think about how you just did in specific situations and in your daily life. What worked well, what will you acknowledge yourself for, what will you congratulate yourself for and what would you like to do next time, perhaps a little differently to improve the outcome.

Over time, you can learn how to ride the rocky bits of life and be comfortable with the notion that while you don't put your hand up to experience the tough periods, every human being goes through them and indeed, they can assist you to develop a strong character and give you the guts to keep going throughout your life. It doesn't matter whether you come from a rich or poor background - whether you had much support - or none. This is your life and you can learn how to make the most of it. You know that your life counts just as much as anyone else's does. You are valued and important and a key member of your community. Just as organisations refine their systems and processes and restructure - so do you.

As John Lennon's song says - *Imagine*. Imagine what you would love your life to be like and set about creating it. Don't give up until it's done.

When you live your life this way, you can learn how to be powerful and a mentor to others. You may not even realise it, but people watch and learn and admire when someone lives their best life and doesn't give up when it gets tough. It gives them the courage to keep pushing through their own barriers. There is a language that comes with this type of person. They are positive and focus on the good aspects of their life and life in general. No whinging for this group and if they do, it is short-lived.

You learn not to allow anyone else to determine who you are or who you can be. Although of course we are all affected by other people and the society in which we live.

I do not want you to take what I say in *Thought Leadership* as gospel.

I want you to think about what I have said in each chapter. Perhaps it may consolidate what you have been thinking about, or it may be foreign to you at this point. You will be able to examine how you have been socialised and conditioned and determine changes - if any - you would like to make in order to achieve your potential over and over again and to contribute significantly and positively to yourself, your community, your society, those you love and to the wider global community. Doing this over and over and over again and all throughout your life is what makes you - YOU - and assists you to unpack the treasures within yourself which may have been latent for generations.

I want you to develop yourself as a human being, develop your inner leader at every level of your mind, body, emotions and consciousness and contribute what you have to the rest of the world, knowing that what you think and know and feel is as important and as valuable as what anyone else thinks, knows and feels. I want you to fill your unconscious mind with many different aspects of life - and to do it often, so that it becomes a friend to you. So that you can experience the wonder of this incredible piece of machinery.

I want you to experience what I experience when I am writing but in your area of expertise. This type of living does not allow fear to dominate and control; it enables you to continue to develop your intelligence in areas that are important and to continue to challenge yourself in many areas - not just the ones you favour and are interested in. Interesting people educate themselves in many areas and if this doesn't come naturally, they push forward until they are comfortable doing it (CBT process).

For the majority of people, the terms inner leader and thought leader are not something they would have ever considered relevant. Indeed, some squirm at the very thought of thinking this way. That I've dared to put you in this category may be confronting. It's not for you, you may ponder; it's for the upper echelons of society. Only for the important people of the world and society - the ones who lead corporations, government, community, institutions. Over the course of your life, these terms may have alienated you as they have done in society for countless others and since time immemorial and this thinking may have stopped you from stepping into your power. Being all of who you can be.

Let me tell you that this isn't so. These terms are for everyone.

You never know what you are capable of until you regularly update your thinking; keep pushing your limits, unpacking who you are. This is what it means to develop your inner leader and how to live your life through a thought leader lens.

There are many interesting components to leadership.

You never know what you are capable of until you regularly update your thinking and keep pushing your limits and unpacking who you are. This is what developing your inner leader means and how you live your life through a thought leader lens.

I have discovered this throughout my life and more broadly since working in the industry. I have had the pleasure of working with many fine leaders, all decent, good, kind people; and when working with them, I have discovered that the process they were learning and fine-tuning in order to take their organisations, their people and themselves to new heights was what we all needed in our life.

Every one of us.

It was confronting to meet so many fine people at this level because I had been socialised to think that they would not be of this ilk. It was a pleasure to be able to assist them to become more powerful in their role and each time I worked with them I learned as much from them as they learned from me.

The learning was clear.

Assisting leaders at this level to develop and fine-tune their systems and processes seemed logical and illogical that the rest of the world did not think it relevant to them. I saw the significant benefits that organisations attained - size or sector not relevant - when they consciously adhered to implementing a systems and processes approach and to always maintaining and monitoring and improving it. I also saw the way that I was able to assist leaders to realise that a systems and processes approach in their personal life made as much sense as it did in their professional life. They were often surprised as to how much difference it made to them and to their family and others in their private life and how it freed up time where they focused on what was most important.

It seemed that this information was not considered relevant to mainstream and this is why I am intent on sharing it because the difference when we apply this approach to our personal and professional life can be phenomenal. Hence, all the writing I do, discussions I have, unplanned chats all around this wonderful world and on any form of transport I happen to be travelling on at that moment. It is exciting and it can change lives. It can help the person to turn theirs around as it has mine over many years and as it continues to do because this way of thinking and living provides me with focus, clarity, determination and the ability to consolidate and focus on what is important to me each and every day, month, year.

> *It seemed insane to me that the brilliance of leadership was considered by mainstream for only those at the helm.*

I like to speak about this concept and link it to the incredible human machine and discuss this throughout the book. I do not understand why we all don't do this. That it is not standard operating procedure for conversations at every level of society does not make sense.

You can see by this explanation and way of thinking and behaving and living your life that the leadership terms which have dominated our way of thinking for far too long have nothing to do with the authentic leadership role or that only those with the title have access to this way of thinking, behaving, operating because they are the chosen few, belong in a workplace or are in the top-job.

The term leadership has been hijacked.

Because of this the majority of us go through life having no understanding of how powerful we can be if we learn how to think and behave differently and to step right into the brilliance of our human machine.

It is a mindset and a way of living, thinking and behaving.

It means that whatever we do will be done to the best of our ability. We will naturally think how we can do it better. We won't take the words of the media or from anyone else who says something for gospel. We will determine if the information we have been given is relevant to us and indeed, authentic. We will support other people to do the same. We will help those less fortunate than ourselves. We will have a global commitment to this and we will naturally want to assist developing countries to get a leg up and to have the basics that we in developed countries take for granted.

Those of us in developed countries will consciously and deliberately stop expecting more and more and stop nit picking when minor things are not done as we expect or have been selfishly conditioned to think that they should be a certain way. We will learn when to simply shut up and say nothing because we can add no value to the current conversation or situation. We will give our ego a rest and at times, knock it on the head.

This is how our life can roll out if we work hard, live consciously and make deliberate, focused, functional, worthwhile decisions. If you take a step back and think about the information in this book, you may become aware that you already think and behave like a thought leader and that you naturally develop your inner leader.

That it may be your standard operating procedure.

It took me much time to become aware of what I am sharing with you and only occurred because of all of the different areas I have worked in and because of my commitment to continually unravelling my incredible human machine.

Observing the human condition is a marvel.

Insights, wonderful insights combined with hard work and tenacity can move mountains.

Human beings can be fragile emotionally and it can be tough to be human, however smart and hard working we are. This is not recognised enough and when it is, it is shoved into silos where we are diagnosed and treated accordingly by someone we think knows more than we do and who will put us on the right path. This may or may not be accurate and this conditioned response is a bit like Pavlov dog's theory. The process can disempower us. This current way of thinking and operating does not understand or respect the incredible capacity that the human machine and infrastructure has to repair itself and to become whole again over and over and over again.

While consolidating the information for *Thought Leadership* I have had a number of insights. Those insights can be confronting because my unconscious mind has pieced together much that I have been thinking about for years or decades. It has assembled them to make perfect sense and now gives me a deeper understanding of what it is that I have been considering and thinking about. It is also confronting and nerve-wracking, because, while the information I have been given makes perfect sense, it has not been filtered. When ideas are quite *out-there* they have to be written in a manner that will engage the reader not alienate them - where the reader will take what they need, think about it and weave it into their Personal Development model (PDM).

The reason I write in a conversation style is because I sincerely hope that it assists my readers to piece their life together and forge ahead. In my life I find conversations fulfilling and valuable beyond belief. This way of conversing is much more personal and I want those who read my work to think that I am talking to just them. I hope you do too. As my confidence and competence has increased, I have developed my own writing style and I like to play around with it. It has evolved over the years. It takes courage to do this because there are those who demand that a writer writes to a specific model and if not, all hell breaks loose. If the book is about thought leadership and developing our inner leader then I must also be brave - as I ask you to be - and forge ahead and challenge myself. It then becomes authentic prose and possible for each and every one of us to continue to unravel our inner leader and to think and behave like a thought leader. Knowing and celebrating that human beings do not have only one potential. That we just keep unravelling ourselves from where we are now and know that when we get this right, it can feel eerily beautiful. We need to give ourselves credit for having the courage to keep pushing forward and moving our mountains.

UPSIDE DOWN THINKING

Not all conversations are equal. Not all conversations are necessary and some need to be stopped. Some people have no idea about what to say and not to say. Some think it's okay to dump their stuff onto anyone who is in their midst. While there are people who say this is fine and encourage it, I see it differently. It can make other people ill and keep the person locked into thinking only about their problems. It can stop them from being aware and developing emotional intelligence. It can stop them from looking more broadly and taking responsibility for their life or seeking the proper assistance to move through their issues and to understand how and why they need to talk about their problems to everyone they run into. I am not advocating keeping it all to yourself and bottling it up. However, there is a time and place for everything. There are many fine professionals who can help us to work out our life issues. If we are lucky enough to have good friends or family members, we are fortunate indeed but we do not want to burden them with every little thing that goes wrong in our life. There are excellent self-help books. When we take full responsibility for our lives and issues, we learn how to develop our own PDM.

There are many examples I could have used for this chapter but chose this one because it displayed precisely what I wanted to say. It encapsulates much in one brief behavioural outburst. The person whose behaviour has been sighted, is a decent person and the example shows how decent, intelligent, well-meaning people make mistakes which impact those around them in ways that if they stepped back and thought about would not want. It shows how much our words and behaviour can impact others and how we can fall into the trap of thinking that our minor issues are far worse than they are. Stuff happens and it passes and much does not need to be aired.

For all of my life I have attended a range of social functions and love them. I love being part of the wider community and

associating with different people. As an adult and as I have built an organisation development career, I have had the opportunity to observe human behaviour in all its forms.

On this particular day, we were sitting around a table, about to share a beautiful meal - contributed to by all, and having a delightful, fulfilling, positive conversation. We welcomed into our midst, a latecomer. A popular, lovely, hard working member of the community who contributes much. It was clear that they had been thrown around emotionally. Rather than taking the opportunity to sit down quietly and process their stuff before they came inside, they chose to do the opposite.

Let's unpack this.

The reason for the problem was that they were impacted by road works. Slowed down by another driver. In addition to this, they then had to look for a car park which seemed to be unavailable. And the ones that were available required that they would have to move the car in 30 minutes or 60 minutes.

This is a luncheon where newly arrived migrants and longer term migrants are being welcomed to the country. We have no idea what they've been through. They may have been through horrific experiences and many still have family back home. They could be struggling financially, physically, emotionally, mentally and have trouble with their new language. Who knows what they are experiencing?

I have found that these beautiful people are positive and grateful for everything that their new country has given them. They cannot understand what people are complaining about because they feel like they have struck gold and are now in a peaceful, beautiful, safe, welcoming country and sharing a lunch with people who really care about them and want to provide them with information that can assist them to live a rich, wonderful life and make good, solid connections.

Let's further unpack this.

The exhibited behaviour, words and attitude may indicate a few things. Firstly, that there was a level of self-pity and that the person felt put upon. It was most likely unconscious behaviour, and they behaved as though the immediate problem was dire and without conscious intention I am sure, this had the impact of dominating the lunch and participants. Furthermore, this behaviour is common in developed countries. Longer term citizens are so use to living in a country that has and provides so much that they want more, more, more. The behaviour exhibited, indicates that we shouldn't be inconvenienced while forgetting that roads need to be repaired and that we are incredibly fortunate to live in a city where that happens; where there are the financial resources for it to happen; that forward thinking and planning has occurred; and where the council and government maintain the infrastructure.

There was a beautiful lunch to be had where we could all share a couple of hours with lovely, decent, kind people and where all problems could be put aside while we participated in friendly, positive banter and enjoyed the delicious food from a number of cultures.

This person has a car - they have enough money in the bank to put petrol in the car, to register it and keep it roadworthy. They are able to drive on roads that are bitumised and have the privilege of driving on roads that are upgraded. Not dust or dirt, not a wet puddle of road but a real road that works very well.

Many people do not have a car, do not have the funds for

petrol and do not have the physical or mental capacity to drive. They are not able to be part of this beautiful luncheon because public transport cannot get them there or because their physical limitation does not allow them to get to the vicinity. They may be working or may not be able to attend because of caring responsibilities.

It wasn't necessary for this participant to say anything about their experience but just enjoy the gorgeous ambience they walked into. They could have just sat down, smiled, said hello to everyone and enjoyed the richness and diversity of the group. Prior to coming in they could have done a couple of things. Perhaps they could have acknowledged what was going on, how they were feeling and allowed the emotions to be there knowing that they would settle in time. They could perhaps have processed the situation and talked themselves through it. They may then have determined that they would be positive and enjoy what was happening while not disregarding how they were feeling but putting it aside until after the luncheon. They could then spend time putting it in context and filing it in their mind accordingly. When the emotions had settled down and they analysed the situation, they may consider that it was not a major problem. It was just an inconvenience in a developed country and that perhaps they would be wise to reduce their stress levels.

There is a much bigger issue at play here and worth contemplating.

We all need to work on our emotional intelligence.

We all need to be aware that there are problems and *that there are problems*.

We need to be socially and emotionally aware enough to behave appropriately in each situation. Much of our behaviour is automatic and from social conditioning and we need to stand back, think about it and unpack what we could do better. If we are fortunate to live in a developed country, we need to take stock of whether we're taking things for granted and expecting more, more, more. I encourage you to think about examples every day where you could have slipped up and change your behaviour and thought process. It takes years to master this and it's never perfect because the mind largely does what it wants to do and we're human - we're going to mess up and probably more often than we would like. But the sooner we start the better. And it is important to acknowledge our self for having the courage to look at our thoughts and behaviour because it can be challenging and confronting to do so.

We can make people ill by dumping our stuff onto them. We don't know what they've been through in their lives or are going through now. We don't know their story. They may not have the skills to

We know that to build a strong functional community, we are an integral part of that jigsaw and our contribution is significant.

work through it and in reality, why should they have to? They might be having a really tough time in their own life. We could be putting a burden and load that is too much for them to handle, manage and process. If it happens time and time again; perhaps a number of times a week, the load can be overwhelming and have a serious, negative impact. Affecting their physical, emotional, mental health and quality of life. Their personal boundaries may not be strong enough to tell the person that they are not a dumping ground and do not want to hear about every little problem.

Facilitators can also help out. They can intervene when necessary because they know that not every conversation needs to be aired. They can gently, firmly, with compassion and respect explain as soon as they become aware where the conversation is going, what the group is now doing and that they would love to have a chat with them in a minute privately. The facilitator can gently stop them mid-sentence if necessary because words build momentum. While ensuring that the person feels respected and valued the facilitator can prevent unnecessary information being downloaded because they know it can derail the purpose of the event. It takes courage to do this because you are risking 'not being liked' but when done with compassion and kindness it can have many benefits for all concerned and can assist in building emotional intelligence.

As human beings, we are personally responsible for our emotional development and need to stand back and listen to what comes out of our mouths regularly. We need to learn how to be our personal counsellor, mentor, best friend, supporter, and collaborator and be honest with ourselves. We can seek professional help and guidance if we find ourselves always caught up in our own problems.

Have you thought about this?

If not, please do.

We need to ask permission before we talk about our problems and not expect the human community to be our personal counsellors or be available 24x7.

I have noticed that women are much more likely to do this than men. I used to do it. Thank goodness for my experience in the corporate sector because I learned many years ago that this isn't what you do. I had the good fortune of a much loved and respected remedial massage therapist many years ago who made it clear to me that he didn't want me to download my problems each time I had a treatment with him. While I wasn't impressed with the message at that moment, he was a great mentor and I never, ever dumped my stuff on him again. It took me a long time to work it out though because I had been socially conditioned to think that this behaviour was normal and with any behavioural change one has to reprogram themselves which takes much time and effort.

When you open your mouth, think about it. Will it increase the ambience in the room with your conversation? Will people feel great because of the positive interaction or will they leave feeling put upon, exhausted and loaded with your baggage? Will it make people feel grateful for what they have and want to be with you because you are a beacon of light and speak positive things?

We're all part of the wider community and every word we speak either builds community or knocks it. This is worth thinking about and practising and taking full responsibility for every word we utter. Think about the type of community we want to live in and then go forth and build it. The health benefit of being positive needs to be acknowledged. It is significant. It is such a pleasure to hear positive news and positive words being uttered. It fills you up and lightens your emotional load. People are to be treasured and treated with love and dignity. We in turn then receive those beautiful gifts when we align ourselves with the right people.

Every day when we get out of bed, we have a choice to make. We can fill each day with positive or negative communication. We can focus on what we don't have, what others haven't done right or how grateful we are to have what we do have. It is our choice and decision as to which one we inject into the majority of our conversations. It doesn't mean that every day is beautiful or that all conversations will be that way or that life will roll out how we would like it. However, it does mean that we make the most of every day and speak in positive terms, even when the other days are rolling out. Those days will pass. Our words impact on us and all who hear them. We need to make regular adjustments to the way we view the world. We can live a rich life regardless of how much money we have in the bank. We can share our knowledge, experience, and learnings with others. When we realise we are not contributing to positive communication or building our community as we would like, we can take steps to change that. We know that to build a strong functional community, we are an integral part of that jigsaw and our contribution is significant.

So, you see it is always how you look at things. How you process it in your mind and then what you allow to escape from your mouth.

3

INFRASTRUCTURE

This is the 21st century. This is an exciting time. This is where technology is taking over our world as we know it. It is being used by all of us. We are dominated by it and this will increase because governments, institutions, organisations are dictating that this is the way of the future. Artificial intelligence (AI) is being added to the mix. People are excited by it, freaked out by it, uncertain about it and some hate it. Without intervention and control it will go unabated and take the human machine to places it may not profit by. With all the brilliance and the possibilities that these new technologies offer, many advances are not assisting human beings to evolve quicker; rather, in many ways they are dumbing us down. Because we are so focused on the scientific method at this point in history and have been since the 17th century, the emotional quotient and key component to humanity is often left by the wayside. If it is the way of the future, then developers need to address this issue and think outside the square.

There is something seriously out of whack here.

Evolution seems to be stuck and technology is on steroids.

Each new generation needs to be taught how to be human - what it means to be human - how that works and how to manage our emotions and mind while understanding how complex the human experience is. How resilient it can be and how fragile it can be coupled with the complexity of it all. We all need to be taught that we can do it and not be dependent on others to fix-us. We can fix ourselves when we know what we are doing. Just the same as we can learn to read and write when we are taught by the right people.

If we allow ourselves to be dictated to by the latest *you beaut* AI development or APP or method we will lose even more capacity than we already have lost. If this does not resonate with you, check out some facts - look around and see how well people are *really* faring in their life and with their physical, mental and emotional infrastructure. Look at the statistics for people struggling with their life issues and see how many turn to licit drugs and illicit drugs to help them to live their life. Look at the number of people who are not taking personal responsibility for their health and turn to prescription drugs to fix them when, if they took responsibility for their health and well-being, many of those prescription drugs would not be necessary - as attested to by those in the know. Look at the increase of stress and anxiety in people's lives. Look at the recent edict from the World Health Organisation's (WHO) policy on burnout.

We are all at risk of becoming the *village idiots* and becoming dependent on anyone other than our selves.

Let's pay a brief visit to the couch, shall we. Lie down, your therapist is waiting. You have a leg injury. Your session includes chatting to the leg and advising it what it needs to do to repair itself. You tell it all about the latest approaches and you are sure your leg will get-it. You know, I know, we all know that this approach is unlikely to repair your leg. The leg just will not get-it. Yet, emotional and mental injuries which impact the human machine's physical infrastructure are still largely treated this way, but with licit drugs added when chatting alone won't do the job.

What if we changed the vernacular so that we talk about emotional and mental injuries in the same way that we talk about physical injuries? What if there is no separation and that we know that it's all part of the same human infrastructure and therefore everything that happens in one area impacts all the other bits?

> *What if we were taught from little that when something goes awry with our emotions or in our mind, it needs attention? The way we do this is by changing the way we discuss the issue and that it is just a job that needs doing. No shame - just a job that needs doing. Project management style.*

Just like the leg injury or bruised toe.

The severity will determine the level of the repair job that needs to be done. Doing this, thinking like this, takes away the shame and fear of expressing our emotional and mental injuries.

It may need a small repair job or a big one.

The way we view repair jobs for our human machine has been out of whack for a long, long time and needs to be brought back into whack.

Since the couch model has dominated we have outsourced our power and while those in this area, I venture to say, are mostly genuinely good people who want the best for their *clients*, it

What if we changed the vernacular so that we talk about emotional and mental injuries in the same way that we talk about physical injuries? What if there is no separation and that we know that it's all part of the same human infrastructure and therefore everything that happens in one area impacts all the other bits?

continues unabated and now with APPS and technology, I fear far too much of our human intelligence and potential brilliance is being outsourced.

If you don't use it, you lose it.

Emotional and mental injuries need to be thought about differently. We know that if left to fend for themselves, these injuries can erode the quality of life for a human being, just as a leg injury left to fend for itself can. Instead of just talking about our emotional and mental injuries and not understanding how seriously they can impact every area of our body, mind, emotions - how when untreated they chip away at our physical, mental, emotional health and cause physical issues - what if we turned all of this on its head and taught practitioners to think differently and trained them differently?

Completely differently.

What if the body knows innately how to heal emotional and mental injuries but we have lost touch with that capacity? What if it needs just a little help rather than the dominant approach that is now embedded into our culture and thought processes? What if, when the right modalities are used, we could have as much success as we now have when repairing physical injuries?

What if we have no clue as to what is really possible with the human infrastructure being able to repair itself? What if at times we intervene far too often? What if, because of the complexity of our human machine that it forgets what to do at times or as well as it used to? What if there are techniques to remind it?

What if we in the Western world have developed an arrogance so deeply embedded in our vernacular and society that we don't even look at other modalities that work and work well, because we think we know it all?

Perhaps there are other modalities that can help our human infrastructure to reboot.

What if, over time we have lost this innate knowledge and need to grab it before it goes away for good and before evolution files it permanently? What if the CBT, other modalities and *the couch* are only one tiny part of a much bigger picture? Why don't we think in terms of emotional and mental injuries being just like physical injuries? Why don't we take a completely different approach?

How have we allowed ourselves to get to this point where we have taken so much power away from the owner of the human machine?

Why don't we give the owner of the body more power in every consultation, instead of assuming that they don't know anything and that they have to pay a visit to the professional who will tell them what to do, how to do it and what to think? What if the professional incorporated a coaching methodology and style with their clients where they inquire and together work out a solution?

A constructive path forward.

Where the professional knows that they are a conduit - rather than having to have all the answers, that they are a participating professional, simply there as a tool to disseminate their information to the client who is paying them a visit. Their knowledge, wisdom, education and experience are valued and important. They know that the determining factor here is to share what they know and to know the person visiting will leave with more information than they came with. They will leave empowered and determined to achieve their goals with some clear goals to work with because of this honest, open dialogue and consultation.

How did we get here? How did we let society get to this point?

What wrong turns did we take when we were at the intersection and pondering our next move? What turns should have been taken? What turns can we take now to get a semblance of balance returned to our way of thinking, behaving, and living?

Evolution is painfully slow and needs a reboot.

Perhaps technology could help here.

However, developing technological advances just because we can is a recipe for disaster.

When we respect people and know that they know much more than they think they know and empower them in every consultation, it is a professional-to-client relationship. It is not the professional-to-patient relationship that dominates and which is considered normal and right. The latter disempowers us - a professional-to-client relationship means, we are equal partners, we learn from each other, we question things and do not behave as we may have been conditioned, where we can remain in a childlike state all throughout our life.

So, it's back to the couch now for some good old-fashioned nurturing and chatting, and making a To Do list, not between a professional and patient but between two equal participating human beings in a community setting, enjoying a cup of tea and a piece of cake. The person who came in for the chat is the one who is in charge of the session and is the one who makes the determination as to what they will do - not the other way around.

At times we need to consult professionals and listen to what they have to say. Indeed, they may be lifesavers, if we have some nasty little issue or a repair job to fix. That is when we need these minds.

But we do not ever need to acquiesce our power to them or to anyone else. We need to be learning all the time.

We need to be thinking and working it out.

We need to be evaluating what has been said and determining whether what that person says is right for us.

Remembering that there are many, many fine and brilliant professionals all around the world with different ways of doing the same thing and that now in the 21st century, we have access to their knowledge and experiences and skills because of technological advances if we are willing to do the hard work. To do the dig. To track them down and to implement our findings and work hard, very hard, to achieve our results.

Always reflecting and always fine-tuning it.

Because of how the human machine works we quickly get used to the way we feel, and because it happens so slowly, we may not even know that our beautiful life is on the way out. Particularly in the Western world - it's just the way it is. It is the way our human mind has been programmed. It is what we must expect as the numbers roll out. That less than wanted way of operating then becomes our new normal. It is accepted without question because it's just the way it is. We don't know how beautiful our life can be again until we have it again - if we ever have it again. This way of living and thinking is bizarre but this is what we have inherited from societal teaching and generational behaviour. When you couple that with the snail pace that evolution rolls out, and now with how technology is changing our lives, and with how the unconscious mind and conscious mind partner, there's a recipe that needs rewriting.

Time that we all learned how to think differently, don't you think? Time that we made thinking one of our main priorities each and every day, don't you think? Time to change the rhetoric to include emotional and mental injuries along with physical injuries in the lexicon, don't you think? Time to teach everyone that we need to give shame and fear thoughts and feelings the boot when we are talking about and living with emotional and mental injuries, don't you think?

Every experience leaves a little mark.

The body remembers, the unconscious mind remembers and drips it through to the conscious mind and emotions where it all plays out in our human machine and impacts our every moment. Our body remembers and is impacted. It is when the little marks add up to big marks that problems can start to occur. It's when the dents are too deep for the physical, emotional, mental bits of the body to automatically repair themselves that the problems can displace our bits. Couple that with poor lifestyle choices, eating badly, not exercising, being in poor relationships, not knowing how to be kind to our self, expecting others to fix it, being so socially dominated by cultural norms that we nearly drown in them, allowing our stress levels to go through the roof and we are setting ourselves up for physical, emotional and mental injuries.

Do you think it's a bit strange that so much compliance and education is required if you want to build a physical structure, but not with the human structure?

A building - small, large, huge - that means you will be driven nuts with the amount of red tape you'll have to wade through and comply with. That the builders will be held accountable to many, many people and every single nut and bolt in the building or in that tiny cottage is there because it is meant to be. You've got project managers, consultants, builders, labourers, all with current trade qualifications. Many people with all types of qualifications are part of the whole process. It is expected. It is legally required. It is heavily regulated. It is fine-tuned and there are always people working out better and easier and more effective systems and processes to make the same structure easier to construct, with less effort and cost to the builder which the purchaser will benefit from.

Billions of dollars are invested into improving systems and processes - the way things are done. In every industry, everywhere in the world. When a building is completed, a maintenance program is put in place immediately because it is known that from the time infrastructure has been created, it will need to be monitored to ensure everything continues to meet current regulations.

There is a plan.

It will need to be monitored and managed and thus a schedule is developed to ensure this occurs.

Why don't we think in these terms before a baby is born and have a key plan to ensure that the baby is given the best chance possible while it is being manufactured and then when born? Why not have a maintenance plan in place and teach this plan and process to the people who care for the baby, ensuring that the child will ultimately take charge of the plan, as they mature and are capable of doing so?

The human machine is beyond complex and brilliant.

It has much to do and needs help to achieve its potential over and over again.

One of the many great things about writing and airing my thoughts is that I continue to learn along the way and insights from the deep reveal themselves. A chapter can change significantly when it is reviewed and as I have said in another part of the book, in a sense it can start to write itself. Words flow - they want a voice and it is something that I may not have considered relevant but it needs to be there. That situation occurred in this chapter. As I have ventured to the end of this chapter it seems to me that in many ways human beings have allowed themselves to be outsourced. We haven't taken control of our destiny. We have allowed technologies and anyone, who says they know what's right for us, to do it. We just sit back and allow it to happen.

That is not how thought leaders live their lives and it certainly doesn't sound like inner leader development.

What is your best thinking on this?

If human beings don't harness technology; if we do not take back some of our power while we can and in the key areas of our life; if we don't stop ourselves from being outsourced to any technology or profession who says it's good for us; then the future will look very different and the erosion of our humanity will continue unabated.

We are capable of so much more.

4

NEW YORK CITY BRAIN

It was such a revelation to me and so astounding that I stopped and just stood there - on the sidewalk next to where I was staying in downtown Brooklyn in the snow, rugged up with scarf, coat and hat with a tiny level of awareness feeling overwhelmed, confused, perplexed, excited and completely in awe by what I had been experiencing over the past couple of days. Emotions poured into my mind and into every cell of my body, with memories from the last time I was in New York City rekindled. My mind was transfixed and filled with questions as to what just happened. There was a

glint of light in my consciousness - way out in the distance though - which brought me to the standstill. I was not going to miss out on this. I needed to work it out in order not to miss an incredible learning opportunity. While a part of my mind was focused on the now - it and my emotions were all over the place.

My whole being was trying to figure it out.

My mind was flitting back and forth trying to construct something to grab hold of so that it and I could understand the incredulity of what I was experiencing in this exact moment. I could have continued on my merry way and had a fabulous day or

I could stop, take it in, process it, try to work it out, benchmark what needed benchmarking and file it all for future reference while learning much more about how my infrastructure works. How my mind had filed these memories and the richness of the experience could be lost. How my mind would file what was happening right now could be lost.

For the researcher in me this was a golden opportunity.

This is what I mean by saying that whatever I do has a leadership component.

There is always an opportunity for learning if I think like this and live my life from this perspective, because doing so provides me with a rich learning environment and I take the *lab* with me wherever I go. Experiences such as this are filled with rich, wonderful learning opportunities and I harness them with gratitude even though they can be confronting and challenging and where I can feel thrown around physically, emotionally and mentally.

This was one of those moments where I could say that all of the stars did align.

It was a magical learning experience and I took the maximum learning from it and with me. I knew that if I continued, my mind would focus on what I was doing and this incredible opportunity to learn more about me, habits that have caused me much angst in my life, and the way my brain had stored memories in New York City which were quite different from how my brain had stored memories in Australia pertaining to the same issue. This was the mind-blowing bit for me. It was the way that my brain had compartmentalised what had occurred in seemingly different segments of my brain. It seemed that my mind had forgotten about all of the changes I had made upon my return to Australia from my last trip. It had jumped right back to *exactly* where I had left it when in New York City.

I understand how my mind works. I understand how I work. I understand how my mind files memories. I understand how stress and anxiety can return me to unwanted behaviours. What I didn't understand was what occurred in New York City at that precise moment, but also the moments that led to this moment in time. It was 12 months since I had been there, had the unwanted experiences, returned to Australia, worked on them, got back in sync, and then standing on the sidewalk in downtown Brooklyn it was as though I had never left New York City, had never worked on them, had never got myself back in sync.

It was as though I had stepped into a revolving door.

I entered at one point, and one moment later - in reality 12 months - I departed at the other side of the revolving door and into exactly the same behaviour. My mind hadn't missed a beat.

Exactly the same as it had been 12 months before.

Habits are what make us.

Each day we get up and get on with it and move forward practising habits unconsciously. We move through our day doing what we've done before. What we were taught by our parents and the society in which we were raised, by all of the people in our life which all links to what we downloaded when we were born. New habits can cause angst and are the reason that many stay with what they know and have always done. It's easier that way, or so we think.

Habits start early in life.

We are programmed from birth. Some say we are brain washed. We all have habits that we have to manage. Some are easy to take charge of whereas others are a lifetime of work where one slip up can see us going back years. And with any habit that does not serve us well, we need to pay full attention to know where we are at with it. And given that this was not a significant issue in Australia and has not been for a long, long time, I expected the same thing on my trip. It was certainly not on my mind because I had toppled the behaviour (once again) and imagined that this progress would also be experienced anywhere I went.

There seems to be shame associated with habits that are related to stress and anxiety. It's put in the mental health arena. I find this weird because stress and anxiety play out in our whole body. There's no delineation and I've no idea how they ended up being slotted into the mental health arena. There is no shame if you have a sore toe or a physical injury, so how did the emotional and mental issues fall into a different category? It's simply an injury of a different kind and one needs to learn how to fix it. And often not even an injury. It's just the body, mind and emotions out of kilter, and the owner needs to know how to bring it back into kilter. How can you possibly compartmentalise the human infrastructure? It all works in tandem and needs all of the pieces to function as it was intended. Just like the building infrastructure - all bits and pieces are put where they need to be in order for the whole structure to work effectively.

Shame is a wasted feeling and emotion and it stops us from taking our power. It gives our power to anyone who wants it and to the professions who have labelled whatever it is that we are feeling shamed about. Waste of time and energy and better if we give it up. If you think about the associated behaviours that go with shame, you'll know for sure that they are all a waste of time and energy. Energy we can use in better ways. Talking about it, discussing it, being free from shame, shines the light on our humanity and we learn that we all have stuff. It's what being human means - we're full of stuff and it's just the way the human machine and infrastructure work. Thinking like this helps to build resilience and if we are not giving ourselves a hard time for something that just happens as part of being a human being, then we can focus on much more important things that bring us the results in our life we want.

Other interesting findings came along after I returned to Australia.

The situation that I needed to manage in New York City did not lessen significantly until I took myself out of the stressful situation and even then, when I returned to Australia, it was still hammering me. It required a reboot and needed to go back to the drawing board to be project managed. Back on track with behaviour management in tow and it took a few weeks before I had returned to normal functioning. My reprogramming campaign has taught my emotions, brain and physical structure how to respond to these situations. I have given those new little synapses a good workout and the new connections have been made, practised and cemented into position, and normally stay where they should be. I am patient and kind to myself because I know all of this takes time, determination, awareness and commitment to self. This gives me the confidence and courage to keep pushing forward.

Seeing myself as the experiment on one level, and on the other the assistant of my own life and experiences, helps me to keep times like this in perspective. It also aids in my

If we do not interrupt habits, stress and anxiety can see our authentic self being lost to unwanted and dysfunctional behaviours that we apply because we are adapting to another us, and it can happen automatically. Whatever habit we allow ourselves to take on, there will be a series of behaviours associated with that.

learning and knowledge if I write down these experiences. I gain much insight from living my life this way, and recording these experiences, provides further insight and clarification. I know that I can reread information from years ago. Pertinent, beautiful, rich relevant information which provides me with benchmarks and more learning and understanding about this complex machine I inhabit. I can tap into those memories at any time I want and see the incredible improvement and difference I have made in my life in whatever capacity I want to view with the video recorder stored in my mind which will replay what I want and when I want it. This of course can be confronting, challenging and at times stressful, but it is mostly rewarding now because of the incredible changes I have been able to make in my life. It is liberating and exciting because I learn more and more about the human condition and while I listen to current dogma, I am captain of my ship and will determine what I take on board and what I do not.

When bits of us malfunction, we do not have to accept that this is it or live our lives from that vantage point when a repair job we decided upon didn't work as well as we had hoped. I learned much from the experience I discuss in this chapter and was in awe of the whole process; and even though I wouldn't have put my hand up to experience it, I am glad I did experience it. It was a rich, rewarding experience to be the observer of it while it played out, knowing that I knew exactly what I had to do, to pull it all back into place.

With any personality type there will be issues that have to be managed and the sooner we work this out the better. It is not right or wrong - it just is. We can adapt our personality and change. The main point is to learn who our authentic self is and then operate from that point as often as we can. Adapt the systems and processes approach I discuss and apply a project management approach to that. If we do not interrupt habits, stress and anxiety can see our authentic self being lost to unwanted and dysfunctional behaviours that we apply because we are adapting to another us, and it can happen automatically. Whatever habit we allow ourselves to take on, there will be a series of behaviours associated with that. Think about it and you will see what I mean. We do not have to allow our DNA to dominate or think that we cannot change because we are hard wired this or that way. Genetics are fluid and our environment makes a huge difference to the way we operate. You may want to look up the term *epigenetics*.

When we know and understand this and take charge, we can change significantly if we put the hard work in, learn how to manage it and don't give up. I have said this a few times throughout this book because it is important to get this into your mind and live from this perspective. It stops us from being dominated by life, society and others, and we can forge ahead and be who we want to be. It certainly helps me to lighten up when I know that if one cog is out of place, then I can fix it. And if I can't I know where I can go to get help. I don't have to live as though I'm the only one on an island - plenty of helpers out there in the big wide world and I determine which ones I utilise. Whether they are from the non-traditional route or the traditional, we can make that decision and allow ourselves to be supported, guided and loved, which is the best place to start from. We can then nurture ourselves and work out our next steps.

I have learned that my mind files things depending on the emotional state I am in.

This has been interesting to observe at points in my life.

> *Benchmarking memories has assisted me to identify this phenomenon and then if necessary and when I am aware, I can refile those memories properly. This process is powerful - I consciously do it - and it allows me to change the memory that wasn't filed as I wanted it to be or correctly.*

Using the process and learnings I have discussed has taught me that I can live a life I love where I focus on what is important to me and where I have learned how to rekindle the lovely, gentle, peaceful memories and good times from my childhood and other times in my life. I allow them to dominate rather than allow the problems of now - which may have been there for a long time or just be a recent visitor - which when left to their own devices can dominate and mask my very beautiful life.

It is always the lens with which I choose to view what is happening that determines the quality of my life and how much I gain from it. The other bits are there - of course they are - however, I choose to live with a glass-half-full attitude. I speak from that perspective as well. It works well and the more I do it the better I become.

Being happy is a skill to be learned and practised and I have and do both.

It is far too easy to get caught up in the tough bits and forget about the lovely things that have happened. Implementing this approach within our incredible human machine gives us power - we take our power back when we are not dependent on other people to make us happy and we can learn how to build on those lovely memories and help them to become stronger and more powerful in our life. We can then learn how to rekindle them when necessary. And we can share in all of these wonderful opportunities that as human beings we will be presented with all throughout our life, where we can learn more about us just as I did standing on that sidewalk in downtown Brooklyn, New York City.

INCREDIBLE HUMAN MACHINE

I feel like standing on a very tall building and shouting all of this out. I feel like the luckiest woman in the world. I feel like the richest woman in the world. It is incredible to have experienced what is possible with the human machine. Just remarkable. Wonderful and exciting. It does feel cloudy. The dominant thoughts and feelings were all-encompassing; they dominated my mind, body and emotions, every minute of my day. They were there for years - many years. Along with everything else that was happening in my life, they kept me locked-in and captive. The danger signals were relentless, pulsating, pounding, oppressive, confusing, exhausting and caused a sense of desperation and hopelessness. Would there ever be a way out of this nightmare and horror? The tsunami kept pounding and as I tried to escape, I was pummelled relentlessly. Danger signals continued to dominate and control my life. They hampered every single step I wanted to take. My mind, emotions and body were put on high alert. Any step forward would be dangerous. This was disabling. Pounding me, confusing me. I had no idea why they were there or what was happening or how I could escape the torment.

Clarity was diminished. Baffled, trapped by it all. My nervous system was shot.

My life force was replaced with exhaustion and everything that goes along with this in the mind, in the emotions and in the body. My true self long gone. As each day passed, the worse this became, until I found myself way back in 2007 and 2008 and writing my second book *Sex in the Boardroom*, building a global business, with many other projects on the go, unable to write sitting up. There was no strength to enable me to do this. I lay down on the floor in my front room with a cushion under my head, looking out the front window to a gorgeous view and wrote the book.

Coming up and out of the horror was just as brutal and confusing as it was then and during the experience. It was there, right in the forefront of my mind and throughout my whole being and it locked-me-in. It was cruel. A despot had taken over my life. The thoughts changed over time as I went further into the confine. They were without clarity, and my mind convinced me that what I loved to do, what gave me great pleasure and filled my life with purpose, deliberation, fulfilment, passion, enthusiasm and energy was no longer what I loved, wanted to do or of any relevance or importance to me or my life. No ability to participate. Locked-down-and-in. These thoughts and feelings continued unabated - the spiral continued tumbling from one thing to another and landed me head first into social isolation which exacerbated everything else I was experiencing. It was horrible. Further barrelling down the tunnel led me to feeling socially incompetent and so ill through every part of my body, emotions, mind, that I could hardly manage, cope or do anything. It was brutal. It was cruel. It was relentless.

Somewhere in the dark fields, this prehistoric machine knew that I was unable to understand or process the truth. That I was incapable of doing so. The realisation that indeed, I had allowed myself to continue down this path and had been catapulted into a seemingly never-ending tunnel of despair. I did not have the awareness or knowledge, and my unconscious mind was not willing or able to release the information I so desperately needed, to be able to stop the deterioration of me and my life as it deepened, and I landed fair and square in hell.

Hindsight, being the erudite teacher that it is, shows me that the human machine I inherited had switched to survival mode in order to preserve me and the human machine itself. That tiny precious little egg and sperm that did its dance all those years ago and the embryo that emerged - its very survival was being challenged. Rather, it was kind. It was a slow journey into it - so slow that I was not conscious it was occurring or really why. On auto pilot, this phenomenal machine - including my conscious and unconscious mind, my emotions, everything in me and about me - was trying to protect me, to keep me safe, and indeed ultimately, was being kind. It was intended to blind me from the horror of my reality where, as each day emerged, my new reality resembled nothing of my former life where I had been vibrant, enthusiastic, passionate, fully engaged with life, had plenty of friends and colleagues, many projects on the go, and a full life I loved and actively participated in, where I kept moving forward, working it out, dealing with human stuff and developing my professional self and global business and writing and contributing to the media, plus was involved in community.

I know that the physiological process doesn't work this way but it helped me to think that my human machine was being compassionate. I was too ill for the other. Too much else was happening which had to be managed.

Fast forward until now and I have survived the vicissitudes of my life, where my life is once again beautiful and peaceful, and I am once again functioning at a high level.

I am free once again.

Free to be me.

How could this be when things were so dire? How could I get myself back to a point where I am better in many ways than I have ever been? How could I regain my health and do it my way?

My stubbornness and determination are what saved the day.

My absolute refusal to give up until I found the right professionals who could help me help myself. It was my unstoppable belief that we really do not have a clue as to what is possible until it is tested, and I had no intention of ever listening to anyone or any professional who hurled labels. Many of the professionals I spoke to did not have a clue. It was their best guess, with the knowledge they had, and that wasn't good enough if it meant that my life as I knew it, was over. I would not allow anyone to determine the quality of my life or my future when they

The notes are a rich source of data and I marvel at what has been possible and what I have been able to achieve by tapping into my human machine's ability to repair itself by providing it with the appropriate tools.

had no clue what was going on or why my health had deteriorated as it had or why things just kept getting worse.

That was why I took charge.

This was not going to destroy my life - a life where I had worked tirelessly to achieve my goals and had far more to achieve before the lights were put out or even dimmed.

It is acupuncture which has given me back my life.

It has underpinned my complete recovery. How do I know this? Because I was working just as hard pushing through the boulders and barriers, pain and angst and life issues, before I commenced working with acupuncture practitioners. I was locked-in, and although progress was made, it was minimal. This modality, coupled with well-chosen practitioners and me leading the way, has opened the gate to me achieving the results I had so sorely wanted, but which had escaped me for years. The treatments are now in their seventh year. While there is no doubt, I have been (and still am and always will be), the project director and manager of my life, it is acupuncture that has enabled my human machine to repair itself, which has enabled me to work with my body, mind and emotions, which has allowed them to return to normal functioning.

Acupuncture treatments have allowed my human machine to rebuild and repair my nervous system.

It now functions normally and better than it has for decades and in some ways better than it has ever operated. An absolute marvel I celebrate each and every second of the day. If I had not experienced this myself, I probably would not have believed it possible.

Insight is always powerful when you are the mug in the middle.

Throughout this near seven-year period of working with acupuncture practitioners, I have been determined to see what is possible and I have pushed and pushed until my human machine has now rebooted from where it was stuck in survival mode until it is now firmly and squarely back to high level functioning and normal.

Acupuncture has been the catalyst which has enabled my human machine to reconfigure and reposition the pieces in the jigsaw that became dislodged.

I have learned much about this modality which has been repairing human machines for centuries and have diligently recorded the information in fine detail for future reference, review and confirmation. This information provides me with clarity and the ability to embark on further changes and consolidation. The notes are a rich source of data and I marvel at what has been possible and what I have been able to achieve by tapping into my human machine's ability to repair itself by providing it with the appropriate tools.

While the above is an accurate reflection and I treasure it each and every day, there will always be required changes and modifications. One must not settle at any point in their life because we can always get to the next point and once that next point has been attained, who knows what's possible? It's worth figuring it out and pushing forward. I will continue to keep pushing through any barrier I consider needs toppling. In many ways, I am better than I have ever been at any stage in my life and who knows where this next bit will take me?

I use holidays as an opportunity to reflect on what I am really doing in my life as opposed to what I think I am doing. Recently, while on holiday to New York City I developed a To Do list with a range of tasks that I would complete as soon as I returned home. This list included improvements in my home and also focused on one particular behaviour I wanted to see if I could topple. It was part of the experience I discuss above and, in this area, I was stuck and my human machine still determined that I was in survival mode. While significant improvement had been achieved there was still much of the old stuff pounding me and it was impacting on the quality of the life I wanted to live.

Armed with my To Do list on my return, I put my plan into action.

Three short months after having been locked-down with this specific behaviour for years, thinking that this could perhaps be one that I may not be able to topple, I could feel the changes that were occurring and that I had indeed broken through the barrier. It happened. I had toppled it and come out of survival mode. I started to feel as I had years ago when I performed these tasks - the energy and pleasure returned and memories from the past flooded back to how it used to be when these tasks were completed. It was beautiful to immerse myself in this again and to celebrate yet another long-term barrier toppled. From being stuck in survival mode for years and years to liberation, and it only took three months to push through this last bit of the barrier.

Another incredible aspect to this breakthrough was the enjoyable behaviours I had not been privy to, while I was in survival mode. They had been there all along, they were being stored but not available to me and acupuncture and the process I used enabled them to return - as though they had never been away.

There is a process that occurs in the mind. A transitional point of exchange.

Sitting on my sofa writing this book, I became aware of a cloudy feeling in my mind. I stopped and took note of what was happening. If I hadn't been working on this book and thinking as much about what to include in this particular chapter, I would most likely have missed the process that was occurring. These moments pass before you know they have even occurred. The physiological process is brief. I became aware at the precise moment that my conscious mind was transporting the memory of how I had been behaving for years as a result of being ill, into my unconscious mind and being replaced by the behaviour that had been resurrected and which now was again normal. It felt surreal and very much like a scene from the movie *Sliding Doors*. I could feel and see it happen. It also felt incredibly exciting to have been privy to this experience and process and something I will always remember and treasure.

I am not normally consciously aware of the physiological process that occurs when a changed behaviour is being transitioned from my conscious mind to my unconscious mind. I am only aware of the results and have written extensively on this topic.

It was the trip to New York City that did it.

It gave me the opportunity to reflect on what was next, and having the break meant I regained energy and enthusiasm to tackle it. I was determined to see if I could push through the rest of what I was experiencing and just see what happened.

When you have been so ill that you can hardly function and then you return to full health, you are never the same person again. Every moment of my life is met with gratitude. Every day is beautiful regardless of how it is rolling out. I allow few whinges and moans to escape my pearly lips because I know how incredibly lucky and fortunate I am, to have been able to climb out of the hell hole. How different my beautiful life could be now. I could have many times accepted that what I had was good enough. My writings confirm I had been improving and what I was experiencing at that point was far better than it had been. If I had done that - if I had accepted *that* success, I would have missed out on all of the incredible next bits I am sharing with you.

The plan for this book did not include the information in this chapter because I did not think that it was now relevant. Reading an article in the *New York Times*, written by a Gen Y, I realised that it is more than relevant. It is essential. While I do not wallow in what has occurred, and am always moving to the next point, this period in my life defines who I am each and every day because of what I experienced and learned. Which all relates perfectly to my inner leader and my thought leadership capacity and approach to life. Reading the article, giving me the feeling that this chapter and information should be included in the book and then writing it (and reading it many, many times), has given me a sense of closure to this horrific period. It has also inspired me to keep moving forward and not to accept the status quo. Unbeknownst, this young writer has given me a great gift.

> *We don't know what our DNA holds. We don't know what treasures lie in there waiting for us to unpack. It is one thing to have been gifted our DNA, yet completely another to continue to unpack it throughout our whole life. All of our life, every second, day, and year is an opportunity for growth and development. An opportunity to further develop our inner leader and to learn, think and behave like a thought leader. We can experience the brilliance of the incredible human machine. Let's not waste a minute of it.*

Revel in it and celebrate it every day of your life.

Make the most of your life.

Love, share, be kind and help your fellow human beings to do exactly the same.

You've got the basics and you can learn how to do the rest.

I am incredibly grateful to be back to where I wanted to be but wondered if that was even possible. I do what I do because I can, because I am privileged to live in the 21st century, in the country in which I was born where all of this has been possible. What more could anyone ask for in their life? I wish you the same.

CREATIVE PROCESS

As a human being I am controlled by the biology of my mind, emotional experience, genetic material, environment, and physical components of my body, plus my individual experience. At times I feel like I am wedged between an old-style printing machine and completely subjugated and dictated to by society and the people in it (often without one word being uttered). While it seems that I am dominated by what I cannot see or ever hope to understand - the unconscious mind and the way my body, mind, and emotions relate - it is hard to attain an outside perspective relevant to me because everyone has their own thoughts and feelings and they are not really relevant to me or how I want to live my life. I need to make a mental note of this.

As I continue to unravel my life and experience on this planet, I am aware that I know little.

The creative process is one such conundrum.

I have grappled with this for many a year - thinking about it, analysing it, working with it, developing it, fine-tuning it and then becoming aware of how it all works and where it comes from. I have heard it spoken about by many highly influential, erudite people. It is often labelled because of its magical and mystical qualities, and hijacked by institutions.

Because of the complexity of the human machine and the mind in particular and because human beings need to be able to explain things, I have listened to people discuss the creative process in a myriad of ways, including referring to it as channelling. Imagine then, after a lifetime of work in this area in one way or another, and after I had been writing for years and thinking about it for as long, the creative process reveals itself.

This was confronting and it took me years to have the courage to say that I understand it and that I employ its brilliance for my benefit in every single aspect of my life and particularly with the writing process where I continue to work with it, explore what's

*The creative process
is another piece of the
human machine that
can remain dormant if
it is not understood.
It is waiting for
the appropriate
environment and
circumstance to be
revealed.*

possible and enjoy it just because I can.

I had mostly kept this to myself because I did not feel accomplished enough to know or possibly understand something which has been the source of so much consternation for eons. Some years later - not that long ago - I had the courage to step out a little further and share my knowledge at a workshop facilitated by an Emmy Award-winning composer, pianist, singer, and music director who is a graduate from the Julliard School in New York City. Given their credentials, I thought this person would know a thing or two about creativity, and coupled with a like minded audience I took a risk and stepped well and truly out of my comfort zone. With adrenalin pumping and being invited to ask questions, I did so. I raised my hand and commenced talking. Articulating did not come easily because of my nerves but I forged ahead. Because I have put myself in this position often, I know that what I say will make sense and I'm grateful for that. My unconscious mind takes over, becomes the driver - says what I want to say and then stops just as quickly when the relevant, appropriate words have been spoken. Knowing that I will make sense is a relief but it does not make the physical or emotional or mental experience any easier and much processing is required after.

I felt I had thrown my hat into the ring and had no idea how I was received because by the time I had finished speaking, my mind had gone blank with nerves. I have no idea what comments were made by the famed performer. There were some comments from the floor. Patronising ones which linked the creative process to being shrouded in mystery. One comment was arrogant and patronising and I was informed by another participant that - *I nearly had it right*.

There is nothing magical or mysterious about the creative process.

Nothing at all.

There are no secrets to it and nothing that we all can't learn.

It is a tool available to us simply because of the human machine we inhabit.

While I can understand why people who do not work in these areas may consider it magical and mysterious, I have learned that there is no magic or mystery involved. My experience has taught me that it is a physiological process which needs to be managed, monitored and cared for. It is the human machine operating at peak level and at its best. Everything needs to be in sync and the person needs to know what they are doing, have their systems and processes in place and tap into the resources they already have while fine-tuning what they know while always improving their skills. Over time one will become more confident and the process matures and you feel you have more control over it. My experience shows that it only occurs when my body, mind, emotions, life, level of adrenalin are in sync. I will discuss the creative process through the lens of my writing because that is how it revealed itself.

Writing is the same as any other profession. The more you do, the better you will become. The more disciplined you are, the more focused you are, the more determined you are, the better you will become. There are no shortcuts. It is hard work. It is a disciplined life and a very focused one at that. Everything I do, every single day of my life, has purpose and meaning. Everything I do in my life is under the umbrella of leadership development. This was a decision made years ago because it doesn't matter how much I love what I do, I am not willing to stay with it if it is not fulfilling. My tolerance to boredom is low and regularly changing professions does not give one the ability to dig deeper and deeper in the same area. And so, I invested in what I knew would keep me interested, enthusiastic, passionate, achieving my goals and contributing to society. Everything in society has an element of leadership development woven into it in some way or other and this is what I do each and every day. Whether I am working, playing, cleaning, relaxing, working with clients, chatting to someone I know or a stranger, there is always an element of leadership to it and it is not uncommon for my mind to get to work and deliver an article after one of these experiences. This gives me a life I love where enthusiasm is close to the surface and where I can work in many areas.

My life resembles little of what is considered *normal* in the 21st century and in an advanced economy. It is a simplistic way of living and I love it. I have chosen to adapt to what is necessary for me to achieve my writing goals. There are upsides and downsides - both necessary to achieve outcomes. Spending a significant amount of time by myself is necessary because that is the way my writing brain works. If I choose not to do this or get caught up in too many other activities, I have learned that my mind will not deliver the words at the level I want. It becomes immersed in whatever else I'm doing and my high level writing ability ceases. So many hours by oneself can be isolating as indeed it was when I was ill and I have to factor this in. It can mean that my conversations are intense when I am writing because my mind is so focused on what I am writing about. I know what the term *absent minded professor* means because when I am in writing mode I am completely focused and cannot take my mind away from it. It has to be this way.

As often as the creative process occurs I am in awe of the whole physiological aspect to it. It is incredible. Most of all I am in awe of the human mind and the way the unconscious mind stores all the information I have fed it over the course of my life. When

I am focused on what I am writing - want to write - it delivers far better prose than I could have imagined. Perfect, beautiful words saying exactly what I want to say. This occurs only when the conditions to allow it are met. My conscious mind being fed by my unconscious mind becomes my personal assistant. The writing process is similar to being at the starting point of a race - marathon, Olympics - any high level race. The body, mind, emotions adapt for that precise moment that we have prepared ourselves for and you cannot stay in that condition for extended periods without experiencing the downside. The downside being that it can lead to burnout and trigger behaviours similar to what are experienced when addicted to any substance.

When I discipline myself to write, it becomes my whole focus for however long the book takes. Each day will be structured to ensure that my writing takes precedence. After I have determined what the topic is and continue to think about it the words start to flow. This is another way the creative process shines. The topic will jump into my mind. I then evaluate if this is important to me and whether I want to invest the time. My intuition is used as a guide and I commence the process. Between 2,000 and 5,000 words can be written in minutes. When I work with a later draft it is not uncommon for there to be 10,000 words to play around with in a chapter because I have just thrown words into that chapter as they have come to my mind and I am not thinking about structure at this point - just relevant content.

This process is not static. The names of chapters change. The content will change considerably. The whole book is often quite different from what I thought it would be. For example, this book is completely different from the webinar it came from, which was delivered to a global audience of senior executives years ago. I wanted to turn the idea that only managers/leaders have access to thought leadership and an inner leader, on its head. Books have a mind of their own. Whatever it is though, I determine the structure and ensure that I am delivering words that are important to me, that share more about the topic being written and that it is worthy of publication. It is a time-consuming process. With the first drafts of chapters having been read a number of times, new ideas emerge. This can be a confusing time because I am not sure whether I am focusing too much on detail, whether I am being pedantic, whether the words are okay, whether the words are at a high level, or whether they need rewriting or deleting.

This is a period where I have to discipline myself to go out socially, ensure I eat properly and put a time limit on writing the book, because by this time the adrenalin is pumping and anything else seems a waste of time. I can't focus on anything else otherwise I lose my train of thought. Having set my home up to support my writing has made it a pleasure to sit and write for hours as the view out of each window is lovely. It is a privilege and I am delighted to be able to observe birds being nourished by my garden and be kept company by their beautiful bird song and activities all day long. I love to see the different species in my backyard searching for insects from my plants. This makes writing an enjoyable experience where I feel connected to nature and the rest of the world. At the moment I am enjoying the backyard trees shedding their leaves ready for the colder weather and covering the backyard with a beautiful carpet of autumn leaves. Other leaves blow in the breeze and fall gently to the ground.

The process I outline continues until I decide that it's enough and I have to consciously decide when the end point for this writing period will be. The issue with this is that the deeper and deeper it goes, the more profound and better the insights, words and detail become. My creativity is high by this point and I love playing around with words, chapters, style, content and meaning. The adrenalin is also high and it is masking fatigue. It seems I have plenty of energy and often the opposite is true. That is what adrenalin does. It masks exhaustion and you can continue to push yourself too much. If I put the writing away at this moment, I will never know what words would have poured out and where that next bit could have taken the book or piece of writing. Hence, the conflict.

The opposite also occurs.

Words can come into my mind and pour out at any time of the day or night wherever I am and then just as quickly as the tap turns on, the tap turns off. The words are there and they are high quality. Often at a publishable level. Just beautiful. When this process is in full swing there is an urgency with which the words must be written. There is a pressure in my brain because I have to write the words down right now. Not always do I have my laptop or a piece of paper and the words will go immediately if I don't start writing at that precise moment. Tension builds as I scavenge for a piece of paper. Any piece of paper will do. Serviettes, toilet paper, tissues. That's it. If I don't get to it fast enough the words dissipate into thin air. This can be overwhelming. If I have been able to capture the words, I put them away to be read at another time. Often when I reread them I am staggered by the quality of the words and as often as it happens, I am in awe of the whole process, and how the unconscious mind continues to know what I want and continues to deliver perfect, beautiful prose which is exactly what I required for the piece of writing.

Given that the conscious mind is said to only hold a few things in it at once, when I am not writing I am doing many other things and forget how the writing and creative process works. It is hard to explain when I'm not right in it. It reveals itself to me as I write again and I adapt it as necessary for each piece of writing. I find it easy to write up to 10,000 words but it is much more complex to write 25,000 or more. I remember when I first started writing professionally, 500 words seemed unattainable. With each new piece of writing the process returns to my mind and as I progress through the drafts, I am reminded of what I have done before with other pieces of writing - particularly lengthier articles. When not writing, it is clear that my mind stores this information for future reference and the filing cabinet of my mind will be opened when I am in need of it again.

Each stage of the writing process is fascinating and illuminating.

At times when I become aware that the chapters are nearing the final draft stage, I will put them aside in order to allow my mind to work on other parts of the book. When I read those chapters again in a few days I can be delighted with what has been written while at other times I find that they are far from complete. Indeed, it is juvenile prose and will require a rewrite or removal from the book. I feel like an anthropologist and it's back to the dig. Over the course of my writing I have discovered that the juvenile prose has more to do with nerves, anxiety and self-doubt about having the courage to write a book and whether it will be of interest to anyone or good enough. Once I settle down, take charge of the creative and writing process and know that I can do it, the other settles down, and the whole process ebbs and flows until it is completed.

When nearing the completion of the book and at the beginning of the final draft the chapters start to write themselves. It is similar to being in an automatic car. I have to be there but much is done with me just being there. Paragraphs start to jump out at me. Chapters need readjusting. Words need to be moved to another chapter, revised, and many are deleted in order to make the writing tighter and to fit with the word length I want for the chapter. While each chapter needs to stand on its own, every chapter needs to be linked and relevant to what I am writing and the purpose of the book.

My intuition is high at this point as is the drive for me to finish the book. It needs to be finished because I am fatigued - the whole process is draining and I have other things I want to do. If I don't take charge now it could go on forever because there is always an improvement or change that can be made. If I find a paragraph that does not seem to fit anywhere but I want in the book, I will edit it until it does fit into the book. I notice that juvenile prose has been replaced by more mature wording and this awakens the memories in me of when I was at university as a mature age student and what was required to achieve a good grade. Until the last essay was handed in and received a pass, I would not have the degree. Same as with the book. Until it's all completed, the book is just a draft. At this stage I am feeling confident because I know what the book is about - I've been head first into it for a long time. While this is occurring, I am discussing the book and its contents with as many people as I can and I take notice of their response and comments. This is reward in itself and encourages me to complete the task in hand. I am excited and encouraged by feedback received. As I often say to people, when I receive this feedback it makes all of the thousands of hours I put into my books and work worthwhile and encourages me to keep doing what I love because of the intergenerational interest and enthusiasm I receive.

As the final draft nears completion it is a pleasant and gentle phase. It has become easy. Chapters are in final draft format and I am having fun with it. Playing around with the prose; changing a word here and there, changing a comma for a full stop or even a semicolon, I am tidying it up - fine-tuning it - and at this point I love reading it because it is nearly complete. It all fits together and makes sense. Every word is where it needs to be. It tells the story I have wanted to tell. It requires far less brain power.

I am being rewarded for having stayed with the process. I am putting the icing on the cake and enjoying every moment of it. I can take a deep breath because I know my hard work has paid off and I am satisfied with the product.

While I haven't spoken much about adrenalin in the chapter, it is a key element to my writing and creative process. Think about when you make a cake - you need all of the ingredients. Miss one of the main ingredients and you won't want to be sharing it with important guests. Adrenalin being a key ingredient of the writing and creative process is exactly the same. If I want a quality piece of writing the adrenalin needs not to be too high - not to be too low - it needs to be just right.

Through my writing I have had the pleasure and privilege of uncovering the creative process. I neither understand how the human mind and all other components of the human machine organise this nor how the unconscious mind formulates all of the information I have entered and then sends me quality prose. No idea at all. I use it because I can. I develop it as my understanding of the process increases, which in turn increases my capacity. Experience shows that my mind goes to work when all systems and processes are in place, compiles what I want and spits it out just as a computer does when it has been programmed. It seems to know exactly what I want and delivers the goods. As often as I have been immersed in this process, I am still in awe of it all - I sit back and think wow, how does all of this work? It is remarkable.

I am glad that I did not believe that it was magical or mysterious and that I did unravel it. It shows me that we can be our own best scientist in every area of our life and that when we do live our life this way, it is much more interesting because you never know what you'll learn or work out next. As each deeper insight reveals itself, you know there are more to come. You just keep digging.

> *When you understand that the creative process is not magical or mysterious and that it is available to any of us, you determine whether it becomes active - no one else has that power.*

This information can assist you to develop and uncover your creative process in whatever capacity is important. It is something that needs to be worked on. Initially you may lack confidence and that is normal. My experience shows that this changes as time has been invested and success attained. Keep chipping away. Once you have arrived at the first stop you can continue to unravel this fascinating physiological process. I have found the creative process to be as important in my personal life as in my professional life. The two are entwined and synergistic.

The creative process is another piece of the human machine that can remain dormant if it is not understood. It is waiting for the appropriate environment and circumstance to be revealed. It's fun to live your life like this where you keep digging and finding out bits about you that you had no idea were there - just waiting to be discovered. Why don't you try it out?

JOHN LENNONS OF THE WORLD

There is no doubt in life that if you are waiting for someone to make it right for you and for all the stars to align all the time, you are likely to be waiting a long time. Perhaps your whole lifetime. If you are waiting for someone to tell you what to do, how to think, how to behave, how to live your life, *the best way, the right way* - there will be no shortage of that. It will happen every single day of your life if you allow it. This can see you living a poorer version of yourself and having no idea what you could really have done in your lifetime. The advice that people shell out is overwhelming, even when they are not asked. These people often haven't got a clue what they're talking about - they do it just because they can. If you allow yourself to get caught up with this, you can see your whole life dominated by people who haven't got a clue, yet they impose their values and beliefs on you.

In the Western world we are dominated by monolithic organisations. Most people do not question what they are told. Imagine that? People not questioning what they are told as to the quality of life they can and will live. It is mind-blowing that we have allowed ourselves to be lulled into this way of thinking, living, behaving, and don't even question it.

Why would that be?

How could that be in the 21st century?

We will all be influenced by many people in our lifetimes. Some good. Some not. I am privy to many of these fine people through the internet, which has now given me a deep global reach. While continuing to learn and educate myself, I am grateful that technology allows me this opportunity. The generosity and richness of the information gained is paramount to me continuing to achieve my personal and professional goals and to staying relevant while learning and understanding more about history as well as feeding my intellect. I am grateful that it is readily accessible. Mostly the people who have developed what

I am viewing will never know how much difference they have made to me and my life and to the rest of the people around the world who source their information. They do their thing because they love it. There are millions of them globally.

Given this, there are many people I could have written about in this chapter.

John Lennon is the person I have chosen but it could easily have been someone like Quentin Crisp.

John demonstrated what is possible and how much influence one person can have in their lifetime which has generational and global impact. And because I want to pay homage to all of

the people around the world who are as generous, hard working, determined, courageous and inspiring,

> Thought Leadership *has been dedicated to them - to the* John Lennons of the world *- wherever they are, past, present, future. These incredible people are the drivers of change. There are many. They leave no stone unturned. They move society forward. They question everything. They work their butts off to achieve their goals. They move through the boulders of fear, anxiety, stress, and uncertainty. Nothing stands in their way. They make it happen because they don't give up until it has happened.*

John Lennon has influenced me since I was a young child. As I have matured, I have viewed his life and what he achieved through a different lens. Not through rose-coloured glasses but through an adult lens; and since working in the leadership development area from a different perspective yet again. I was a child when John Lennon toured with the Beatles to my hometown in Australia. Too young to be able to attend the performance; it has been said that this part of the Australian Beatles tour was one of their largest audiences. Given the media coverage I was still able to be involved in the excitement - I have memorabilia from that time and I can reminisce.

Lennon was not born with a silver spoon in his mouth. He was one of us. A hard working boy from the blocks. He did not come from a family that would have assumed this type of success. He worked tirelessly to achieve his goals. He learned what worked and what didn't work. He put the long hours in. He knew all about frustration, success, happiness, sadness, as well as not having a clue what to do next. He knew about sycophantic personalities hanging off his every word - parasites waiting to suck the life force out of him for their own selfish purposes. They are those, who have no intention of giving anything, but steal ideas, knowledge, money, energy. The hangers-on in the world.

There would have been many times that John would have wondered - just like you and me - why he bothered with it all, when things were going so badly. When the media and other key figures were so against him and what he was aiming to achieve. People like this are ahead of their time and some will do anything they can to bring them back into line and make them conform to the current societal dogma. At other times, no doubt John would have been flying high because of the way life was flowing - seemingly easy and beautiful - when everything was falling into place the way he wanted, when the stars were aligned. The point here is that human beings need to look up to people - we need to be inspired by people. Then we need to take personal responsibility without hopping on board someone else's life and forgetting we've got our own to develop and unravel. We need to stand in our personal integrity and not put these powerful, influential people on a pedestal because in every sense - other than their celebrity and media-placed status - they are exactly like you and me. They are human beings with all the needs that human beings have. Except because they have been shoved on a pedestal, they have far more than you and me to deal with. Far more problems and issues to manage; celebrity being one of them; success the other; people the other.

This committed musician was a thought leader before the label was embedded in the vernacular, and continued to unpack his inner leader with passion and fury. He had fervour and was relentless. From what I have observed in media coverage and from his writings, music, interviews, he often had no clue about what to do or how to do it or even what his next course of action would be.

He was a complicated human being and those who knew him attest to this aspect of his personality. What John didn't do was give up. Tenacious, stubborn, impatient, intelligent, thinker, determined, kind, generous, loving, patient, hard working,

This committed musician was a thought leader before the label was embedded in the vernacular, and continued to unpack his inner leader with passion and fury. He had fervour and was relentless.

deliberate, and purposeful, which are all great and necessary qualities for anyone who wants to succeed. He had an attention to detail and to achieving his goals. His ambition was limitless and the more he did, the more he wanted to do. He lived where he needed to live at any given time, knew the importance of living in an environment that would support his life's goal and knew that if he wanted to succeed, he had to take time out to think, to have solitude, and to be surrounded by people who would support him. Many people did not support his goals, yet he forged ahead and did what he believed was right. He had his partner, lover and wife Yoko Ono next to his side for years. He had his kids in his life, and collaborated widely with people, local, national and international.

John Lennon could have allowed his frustration to take over, allowed his failures to take over and whinged and moaned about what wasn't right. He could have blamed society, government, his past problems, his current problems for not being able to achieve his goals. He could also have lived a very ordinary life and had a much easier time of it than he did. He may have never known what he had been gifted by his forebears. How tragic that would have been for him and for the rest of us. Whatever he did, I am sure he would have been successful; but he chose to do what he did, which made him a superstar in the world's eyes.

Inheriting DNA is one thing, unpacking it is completely another, and it is entirely up to the owner of that DNA.

No one forced him to do that.

He did it because he wanted to and because he was driven to do so. He continued to dig deep, to evolve as a human being, as a creator and artist, as a man, a father, a husband, a friend, and colleague; and he shared his knowledge and learnings with millions of people.

He certainly gave his human machine a good workout.

Few people reach the heights that John Lennon did.

He is seen as a demigod, put on a pedestal.

The twist here is that we put the *John Lennons of the world* on a pedestal. We allow the romantic feelings - just like the first stages of a love relationship - to take over and we lose sight of the real person.

We need to unpack all of this given the book that it's in.

You may want to think about a few things such as: Why are human beings besotted by other people who they think are better than they are? Why do they think that celebrities are so different from them? Why do people purchase similar clothing to what celebrities wear? Why do people try to emulate celebrities?

How does all of this fit into developing our inner leader and to think, behave and live from a thought leadership perspective?

The simple answer is - it doesn't.

When we are putting people on a pedestal and idolising them, when they take our breath away if we are close to them or at a concert, when we wear similar clothing, we lose sight of reality and forget that these people are human beings and are as complex as us. We are not conscious of the fact that someone at that level has far more issues to deal with because of people like us who put them on that pedestal. It is most likely not with intent and unconscious nor is it wanting ill for them, but nevertheless when we do this we are only thinking about our needs and what that person does for us and how they make us feel.

When we have put people on that pedestal and the tide changes and they are no longer viewed highly by those who put them on the pedestal - rightly or wrongly - there is only one way off the pedestal and that's down. In the Australian vernacular this is referred to as the *Tall Poppy syndrome*.

Why do we allow ourselves to be seduced like this and put other people on a pedestal?

Why do we need to do this?

Why do we allow ourselves to lose a sense of our own individual selves, identity and power, lose sight of our goals and aspirations, and stay stuck in a mode that is not conducive to us unpacking who we are because it takes far too much focus off our life and is put onto someone else?

Why don't we spend as much time working on our own life as we spend idolising someone else?

If this resonates with you, you may want to consider how this type of behaviour could impact someone if they do this quite regularly throughout their whole life.

I wonder whether it is a way of avoiding being human and dealing with and processing our human stuff because we either don't know, haven't been taught, or it's just too hard and complicated? Or it could be too tough to get up that *close and personal* to our own stuff.

I wonder if it is a smoke and mirrors approach to life.

Whatever the reason, we do ourselves no favours and we certainly do those we put on a pedestal no favours. It is understandable when we are kids and adolescents but not when we are adults.

Many people idolised John Lennon and therefore much of the real person would have been missed by those who knew him or met him. Very few people would have known the real John Lennon - even the ones closest to him because of their rose-coloured glasses and being in awe of someone so famous. When we allow ourselves to be taken over by emotion and wear our rose-coloured glasses, we deny the person their humanity. They are an object of our passion and glorification. What we do is unwittingly selfish. We take away the person's right to live their life as we do and as they want to, and in some ways, we can make their life hell. We do this under the guise of loving them. A product - a commercial icon - just there for our own needs.

The real person isn't even in the equation.

If you aim to attain this level in society you will have a very different view of it all. What you will find is that you will work harder than you ever imagined and you will be faced with issues that you wish would just go away. You will be faced with people that you wish would just go away. As well as very good people.

Living like the *John Lennons of the world* is fraught with obstacles. How would you know who your real friends are, and how would you spot the sycophants who are there to take you down, to take advantage of you and are only interested in what you can give them?

It is important to be aware of all of this and to realise that things are not always as they seem. We would be wise to sit back and think about how hard one would have to work to get to this level and by doing so, we would have much more respect - not blind love - for what they have achieved.

For 40 years now, Yoko Ono has continued the work of her husband and the father to her son. She has worked tirelessly in his name and for the causes he worked on throughout his life and career. It was in 2015, while in New York City, that I was fortunate to be there while celebrations were being held for John Lennon's 75th birthday. Yoko Ono organised a *stand-in* in Central Park's East Meadow. Her expectation was that if between 6,000 and 10,000 people gathered - stood in unison - while displaying the peace sign, a record would be made and would be entered into the *Guinness Book of Records*.

While the record was not broken and while it was not entered into the *Guinness Book of Records*, it was a privilege to be there amongst like minded people and to see the intergenerational mix. It was surreal as I walked through Central Park to locate the East Meadow, which by the way is just across the road from where John and Yoko lived and where Yoko still resides when in New York City. Strawberry Fields is also close by. The John Lennon educational bus was there, which provides tuition in music to children who otherwise would not be able to afford it.

In addition to this, I felt privileged to be able to attend a *Retrospective for John Lennon* orchestrated by AFA Gallery in SoHo New York City, where a number of original paintings and drawings were on display for the 75th birthday celebration.

John Lennon would have continued to make change in the world in the areas he believed were important. His life would have ebbed and flowed like all of ours do. He would have had tough times and wonderful times but there is no doubt in my mind that whatever he did, he would have made a huge difference. He would have continued to evolve and his art form would have adapted to the times. Who knows what other areas he would have conquered and moved into? Who knows how many different sorts of people he would have collaborated with and where he would have lived and worked? The technological ability of the 21st century would have impacted him and provided access to countries, people, mediums he had not contemplated. I wonder how he would have used social media to deliver his music and message. Imagine the campaigns he would have been involved in. Imagine the political commentating he would have orchestrated and the social issues he would have tackled.

The lyrics to *Imagine* are easy to find on the internet.

Let them play in your heart as you read this book and let them be embedded in your mind. Let them impact you when you need support, guidance and love and when you either feel lost, exhausted, or just need that little extra push to do what you would love to do. Don't ever underestimate or think that what you do is not big enough to make a difference. No matter how small you think your contribution and impact is, when we all come from this change perspective, it makes a huge contribution to the world.

We can be inspired by the John Lennons of the world and be fuelled by our own passion and enthusiasm for what we truly believe in and then get into action to achieve it while living our fabulous, amazing, best life.

John Lennon's 80th birthday will be celebrated on 9th October 2020.

There will be celebrations globally and much activity in New York City.

We can all take a lesson out of John Lennon's life story. We can all learn from the incredible tenacity he displayed throughout his whole life. We can display those same qualities in our lives.

John Lennon did not live his life looking through rose-coloured glasses or through a can't-do lens. He and the *John Lennons of the world* live their lives through a can-do lens, live it according to their own values and principles and forge ahead relentlessly. We can all do this and if it is not in our nature or if we have been socially conditioned not to, we can learn how. We can be inspired by the *John Lennons of the world* and be fuelled by our own passion and enthusiasm for what we truly believe in and then get into action to achieve it while living our fabulous, amazing, best life.

8

INTROSPECTION

Do you regularly and constructively sit and reflect on conversations that you have had with people when you are in a social or any other situation? Do you gain knowledge about yourself and others with this process and then make necessary adjustments to behaviour, friendship groups, social connections, and business connections? Do you take too much responsibility for other people's behaviour? Are you aware when you are in sabotage mode? Do you correct yourself consciously (in your mind) when you need to? Do you allow other people to have their say and opinion but not take that on board without thinking as to whether it is relevant to you or your life? Do you assume other people know more than you and therefore you should do what they say? Do you naturally do what an expert says and think the way they say you should think? Do you regularly fine-tune and edit the information you have in your mind before you allow the words to leave your mouth?

Are the above concepts something you think about and consider regularly and update?

Why do you think so little investment is put into the human infrastructure before, during and after a new incredible human machine is hatched? Why are we so highly regulated in every area of our lives, yet with the most fundamental, important part of the whole equation, we are not? It is bizarre. We are given no education to do one of the hardest things we'll ever do: to raise the next generation. I do not want governments to take over this role and dictate how parents should raise their kids. That's not my idea at all. But I want people to have a clue about what they have to do to raise functional kids.

It starts right at the beginning - before the beginning, in fact.

We are not a clean slate when we are born.

In us, there is always that happy, carefree gorgeous little baby, toddler and child and that scared little kid when being told off or disciplined. We are the adolescent and we are then the adult. Those experiences are always with us. They don't dissipate as the numbers roll by. We came from those original cells. It is that history which has made us. We are not aware of how much our earlier experiences influence and dominate us. We are a product of before, while the now is rolling out and while we contemplate the future. We try to make sense of this in the present moment.

Why aren't we taught how to manage our emotions, and learn from a young age how they impact our whole body? Because of this lack of awareness, we are led to believe many things that are not true. You cannot separate the mind from the body, or the emotions. How can we? Everything that happens to one part of the body impacts the rest.

I often feel like a puppet on a string and know that I am told what I need to know which often is quite different from the reality.

Do you often wonder what this thing called life is all about?

I do, and I contemplate it often. Life is anywhere between incredible, peaceful, gentle, beautiful, magnificent, overwhelming, complicated, confusing, challenging, scary, and brutal, and often I have no clue what is going on or why.

Each generation brings new ways of thinking and behaving.

Earlier generations often cause friction because they do not want to move forward and would rather stay where they are. They think that the changes are not necessary and are determined to hold onto their core beliefs. They can hold new generations back because they think they know best. Later generations will push forward because they have to. They will take society to the next level. It is not then surprising that many of us wonder what it is all about.

All advances are not equal and all advances are not necessary.

If you and I don't make change, then who do you think is responsible for making the changes we want? If you and I don't make change, then do you and I really have any right to complain if things aren't going our way? If you and I are not willing to put the hard work into changing what we don't want or like, who is responsible?

When I am in worry mode it seems that my worries and anxieties join forces and it can be difficult for me to gain clarity. It can feel like a tangled ball of wool. These periods are stressful and confusing and I can operate from dysfunction and the old stuff can return to the fore. I need to pull it apart, untangle it all and think about it and work out how I can move forward. Breaking the issue into small bits works well - a professional gave me this information years ago. It has paid dividends. I find that the surface concerns generally have nothing to do with the real issues that need to be addressed.

What are your thoughts on all of this? What is your way of

working out your world? How often do you do it? Why do you do it? What do you need to do to move it all forward? How do you get through the bumpy bits of your life? And why do you do it? Are you aware of all of this? If not, what do you need to do to become aware of it?

The human ego is interesting.

I became aware of it as I climbed the corporate ladder. I noticed that people treated me differently. They saw me as important and treated me that way. They listened to my every word. Some seemed nervous in my presence. I was put to the front of the line whereas before I wouldn't even have been in the line. I had been elevated to a higher position in society. It was a bizarre experience. As I became aware and gained clarity that I had allowed myself to get caught up in this, I also found that a part of my psyche loved it. As a result, I took charge, stopped it and changed the ways in which I operated professionally. I do not think I am better than anyone else and I do not want to be elevated by anyone. The upside may seem exciting for some; however, the downside is no fun at all. Only one way down from the pedestal. Authenticity is at the top of the ladder for me. Not ego or other sabotaging behaviours.

Have you thought about the profession you have chosen? Do you love it and can't wait to get out of bed to start each day?

Does it fulfil you and make it hard to take time off? Or are you involved in a job where you go and do what you have to do and then live your life? If it's the latter, why would you do that? I understand that we have to pay the bills. That's a given. However, if we do this all our life, then we need to take stock of it and ask ourselves: why? It has huge ramifications and living this way can erode our human infrastructure. If you are in a role that doesn't fulfil you then it is up to you to have other areas in your life that do. Sometimes we do have to work in roles that are not what we would like. However, if that is the case there are many ways we can ensure that we fulfil ourselves and that our lives are rich and fabulous.

On the other side of the coin, don't believe the myth where people say that if you love what you do then you never work a day in your life. That is a fallacy. Any work you do requires physical, mental and emotional energy and if you love what you do, you will put more energy into it. Burnout and high levels of stress and anxiety are the result of not giving yourself a break and not respecting what you need.

If you have an account with an organisation - let's say a bank - and you ring them to discuss your account, you expect them to know exactly what has happened and the outcomes. You expect - demand - that their systems and processes for recording your information are as close to perfect as one can get. And if they do not comply, there is *hell to pay*. You are unlikely to ever speak to the same person when you ring. It is because of their records - their systems and processes - that they can tap into that knowledge within seconds.

Here's the twist.

> *If we expect such compliance from organisations and the way they manage and build their infrastructure and if organisations invest so heavily into developing these, managing these, improving these, then why as human beings are we not taught that effective systems and processes are just as important in our personal lives - not just our professional lives? Why are we not taught this from a young age and then follow this process throughout our whole lives - managing it, fine-tuning it and developing our selves along the way?*

Given that our current society is heavily dominated by scientific methods then let's all become our own best scientist. Let's emulate brilliant scientists who are humble, hard working and always working it out. The ones that don't get stuck in their ego or think that they know it all. They are always learning, always thinking and defining their process and hypothesis. Always questioning and updating their skills and knowledge and linking it to their area of expertise. They tell us that their hypothesis is current. They advise that it is likely to be toppled at some stage. If you venture back through history, you will become aware that there have been millions upon millions of hypotheses. And if you dig a little deeper you will learn that some have taken the human machine to new levels while others have detracted from benefiting the human machine and been toxic to it and to humanity.

I have spoken quite a bit about benchmarking memories in the book and will give you a little more information in this chapter. I find it a valuable technique and use it often. I return to former situations and experiences and do this to assess how I am with a particular issue. Perhaps I want to be aware of where I am with a behavioural change and observe where I am now with it as to how I was at a previous time. I consciously take myself back to the situation I want to remember and then the visual of that whole experience is replayed in my mind. The information has been stored in my unconscious mind in minute detail and I now have access to it again.

No magic. No mystery here. Just the incredible human machine at play once again.

The physiological process at work, my having learned how to tap into this available resource where I have learned how to manage it, recover it and fine-tune it, have given me the confidence to increase its capacity. This process has taught me how to tap into the visual bit of my mind, to explore and expand the creative process and my intuition has increased as a result.

What we know is that the status quo in life is always changing. We know that adaptability is key. We know or should know that the near impossible is possible when we continue to unravel who we are, when we continue to unpack our human machine and focus on developing our emotional, physical and mental selves. We need to break down how we have been socially conditioned and stop listening to people who say it is not possible. It takes courage to unpack and develop our authentic selves. When you allow people into your real world and where you dare to reveal who you really are, you can open yourself up to criticism, to being judged and being side-lined. This is something we all need to learn how to manage.

It is a wonderful thing to be alive in the 21st century: so many possibilities; so many options.

For me, it is a great privilege to work in the area of leadership development. Everything that happens in life - everything I experience, discuss, view and think about - has a leadership component. This means that there is a never-ending source of delight and inspiration for me as I continue to unpack the incredible human machine. I am able to continue to live a wonderful life where I can work and share my knowledge and experience globally. By doing this, I feel fulfilled professionally and personally. I also know that I have not wasted my life - that I have contributed much in many areas in order to assist people to do the same. We need to make the most of it all.

Don't let other people determine your future in any area of your life.

Be you. Dare to be you.

It is your life. Live it your way.

Do with it what you want.

The deeper you dig, the deeper you dig and the more rewarding and interesting your life can be. The more treasures you can uncover. Sprinkle it with gratitude and humility and compassion and kindness. Daily introspection is essential to every human life and a key element to assisting you to unpack your inner leader and to think and behave and live your life through a thought leader lens.

When you have this level of introspection and live your life this way, you open up your life to all sorts of possibilities that you may otherwise not have considered possible. When you underpin this by looking after your health and taking full responsibility for it, you are more likely to focus on building, developing and living your best life more productively and pleasantly. When you do not allow society to dictate to you regarding the numbers of your age and how you should be living according to those labels, the opportunities and possibilities available to you throughout your whole life are incredible, inspiring, powerful and endless.

www.ingramcontent.com/pod-product-compliance
Lightning Source LLC
LaVergne TN
LVHW040154080526
838202LV00042B/3148